ROMANS

ROMANS / SNOWMARE

CAM SCOTT

ARP Books (Arbeiter Ring Publishing)
205-70 Arthur Street
Winnipeg, Manitoba
Treaty 1 Territory and Historic Métis Nation Homeland
Canada R3B 1G7
arpbooks.org

Design and layout by LOKI
Printed and bound in Canada by Imprimerie Gauvin

"In An American Country" originally appeared in *The Capilano Review*.
"Zones" originally appeared in *The Nervous Breakdown*.

Sections of "ROMANS/SNOWMARE" have appeared in *Sleeping Fish*; in *Mirage #5*; and in *I.D.I.O.T.*, with a Slovenian translation by Monika Vrečar.

ARP Books acknowledges the generous support of the Manitoba Arts Council and the Canada Council for the Arts for our publishing program. We acknowledge the financial support of the Government of Canada and the Province of Manitoba through the Book Publishing Tax Credit and the Book Publisher Marketing Assistance Program of Manitoba Culture, Heritage, and Tourism.

Canada Council for the Arts Conseil des arts du Canada
MANITOBA ARTS COUNCIL CONSEIL DES ARTS DU MANITOBA

Canada Manitoba

LIBRARY AND ARCHIVES CANADA CATALOGUING IN PUBLICATION

TITLE: Romans ; Snowmare / Cam Scott.
OTHER TITLES: Poems. Selections | Snowmare
NAMES: Scott, Cam, 1985- author. |
CONTAINER OF (WORK): Scott, Cam, 1985- Snowmare.
DESCRIPTION: Poems.
IDENTIFIERS: Canadiana (print) 20190117877 |
Canadiana (ebook) 20190117958 |
ISBN 9781927886274 (softcover) |
ISBN 9781927886281 (ebook)
CLASSIFICATION: LCC PS8637.C6833 R66 2019 | DDC C811/.6—dc23

MIX
Paper from responsible sources
FSC www.fsc.org FSC® C100212

CONTENTS

ROMANS First notebook with the pen Jen gifted me and I could hardly write more gladly, gliding word to word in alphabetical legato. But one can't scratch in advance of landing. We rely upon our foes. Tomorrow's forecast is an aid to fashion. She left the spare key in a pile of rocks. I'll dig for that admission. Placed on death watch by a stranger at the docks, I counted ducks instead of lucky stars. More idle than an elongating limousine, more languorous than landed fish. The less of me there is to hate the more you kick at recollection. Gazing uptown, counting crystals in the storefront, everyone agnostic in good health. A flavour dream, an almond tree aflame, and other roasted omens. The day after Halloween on Maujer Street, sidewalks littered with wigs, I was walking so well that my legs wouldn't let me arrive. I knew then what I had already. When the city is but snack dispensaries and vintage stores, then will the centre burn its surplus, clamouring to queue behind a new USSR? I offer your depiction to the stars, as near, or far, as I can reach. His last request was for a toothpick, oral mutineer. Flared eyeballs, blue lapel. An anatomic heart caught in the throat. Thursday's disaster, draw blinds billowing like barcodes in the rare books, four of us plush mischievous in felt chairs, not a fellow traveler in sight. Bought Ubu buttplug, waddling woodblock. Bumble-bauble with a target on its chest. Feeling litigious, so eschew me. Can't suppress a sneeze in such close corridors. What kind of clown is that? Ill-clad, clogged orifice; a cloying quaver in the voice. A cotton scepter crowned with wax, no body odour here. Nor there. It's a question of balance. If anyone compares Pere, pear-shaped, to Herr President, I'll pull my hair. Les non-dupes errent. A parent trap, or primary forgive-me-not. Like Alice, Toklas, Acker's custard, do I leave a single recipe behind me as a testament? History fucks itself, first in claymation, then as puppet theatre. Words you can't spell without fenestration: abdomen. Defenestration. Death notices outpace the cargo they would consecrate. I am very sad for comedy. A letter to the editor dashed-off abashedly, I'm sorry for your loss. Yes, very sad. The help-lamp gives a whole new meaning to mood lighting. I would rather a dull razor, so I don't sprout blood a minute later like a fleshly sieve. The tree looks that way for a reason, it has roots beneath the stage. Flat affect, bushy head. Food cart to be continued. Actors, painters, lesbians, sometimes all three. A rhapsody in ROYGBIV. Nights I would lie awake and savour the thrum of the street. A plane passing over a train above construction made a solid chord so powerful the cyclists stopped in awe. The city is a problem of transcription, to a point. LED garlands score the branches, a phantasmagoric quorum of dead enemies in lights. Percussive aftermath of the collision, dragging detritus behind its festive caravan. Happening chicken. Not traumatic. Think of it as one thing following another. Every painting called 'Untitled' in a pile. Every opinion in a pie. An open-palmed messiah in a bathrobe bled crumbs to the leaky bank and back. The love-loss hobbled him, we gobbled gory suds along the wake. Movement agglutinates, a church is like a permanent parade. The party is a motile ceremony. Meat is murder, surely you'll permit me that. The meeting has a negative capacity, boring a portal through the ceiling. Motion cloning frame to frame. Mute matter with the memory of animation. Blown leaves down the BILCO Hatch, blue lingan cries. The most exquisitely timed breakup letter in the history of watercolour. Organ music, an anthology. The window is what one omits. On hold for one half-hour, Chic's São Paulo pressed into my ear. Carcinophonic, as the phobia would have it. But I own this record, why endure it elsewhere? Your new lip balm burned me. What's the play? A mouldy body in the miniature terrarium. It turns out one can't cordon rot, or even decompose without intent. Another phallic fungus on a string gives me a tummy ache, to think of a plasticine turd just fossilizing in the gut. Impinged upon by overarchitecture of, plaint gleaned across the gallery. Cleaning the eaves. Alterations are obtainable by changing, in consideration of the whole design, the following key features. Haunted headphones, missing batteries. I'm looking at these paintings, waves of paisley, a lenticular dessert, doing a soft shoe for the bathroom. Like the best of us, I am a dupe for backward masking, blip obliterate the breaks.

SNOWMARE

Materials pertaining to
The watched pot never boils
It spilleth over

As for meanwhile I'm OK.
That I never was surrendered to
But reprimanded

In cherishing the cauldron
On account of others, one may come
To breathe its fumes exclusively

A foil boat floating atop an aluminum sea
Entrails effluvium
We thrived on it
The torturous last season
WHATS UP

Writing. Doing stuff.
Of blue paint flaking off the pillar
Brushed by forking ferns
The driftwood salvaged doorstop
Or my neighbour praying over
Jars of rice amid the mice
In her garage

I guess considering it is to be alive
That we must never blunder
I will take my knocks
Stay buoyant
Write my books
Which spell resistance
In an egoistic & restricted sense

Credit the social network
For a papular eruption
In a public square

The pigeons riot everyday—
Patriot ducks form breadlines, and they mate for life.
Most hacktivism is just fucking around.

For I am ready to get what I deserve
In that order
And to rock the house as a priority

If not as a career.
I couldn’t wait to grow into my shoulders
And start slouching for effect

Which is too thrifty to suffice
As an excuse for just how free we are—
I don't shave during the playoffs, but I wax

Before a date. Promise of consummation.
"I have a timeline for my goals."
"I know people for sex."

If when we die we go to where they fit
Those tiny ships into those tiny bottles
And the meaning into words

Spent sauce into the world. Wrote postcards
Each day that you were away and mailed them
In the waste bin down the street.

Leaving the fountain with wet hands
He slapped the surface of a January cold
And stuck. Indoors dissecting gonads
I was galled to find curled up inside

Homunculus. That all my life has been
Shambolic but I never broke the skin.
The regulation handprint fits a glove.
How we flatter the polis with song

His piteous sobs wracked the outfit.
'Tragic' the word lays bare
How little our mauve feelings matter.

That words could be the greatest pleasure
In the world seems an affront to sex
Which has precisely such a limit.

On the other hand, try using words without
To minister to your community
A sign, which means the same as sacrament
Those terms are interchangeable

Love that occasions designation
For the sake of unity and the beauty of synchrony

Inhaled him through a veil of cotton
While he held me like a handle.

"I am too good to be abstract," he said.
"I am too hurting not to be explicit."

ROMANS Do faces have headlights, or windows? I've never slept the night before a trip, too busy planning about packing. Dark chocolate parching, an excellent source of magnesium. The stream of everlasting life is owned by Nestle, too. What's on tap in the master bathroom? I'm so thirsty I could suck a faucet. If we're going to have to suffer anyway, why wait? One must live equal parts in heaven and on earth. Is freedom a state or a road? "The law does not construct a subject who simply and unequivocally has a desire, but one who rejects its desire, wants not to desire it." Her dad was a cop or something. There were bagpipes at the funeral, no one wept. I'm a vicarious sensualist, lingering near second-hand smoke as one might have loitered at the mall. All atmosphere is lightly used. Nothing originates. Made with natural flavours, derived from natural sources. Breakfast at Tiffany's, bus depot Thunder Bay. The lion's mane has fallen off but carries on in name. Catching cobwebs in my hair, a silk proximity to skin, I bless the sickening illogic of it all. A putrefying factory or mobile lobe, courting contempt foot over fossil. Am I that bowl of brains, a swollen bag of blood? But then you never see a corpse that isn't made up on TV. Slept past the water pipe emporium. Catastrophism is "for all"—no nukes, a meagre veganism. As she neared moral perfection, her to-do list dwindled to a few pressing mistakes. The region's richest silver mine reduced down to a supple islet. A panoramic view inside a rock. O Sponge, your own name is a verb—conatus, indifferently sexed. One can't mix poetry and politics without theft of necessity. Start with the ideas then. Nostalgia has no bearing upon justice: neither as fidelity to an event, nor as speculation on the resurrection. Imagine a world in which one may adequately mourn. The meadowlark tried in its way. A tradition that extends toward Antigone. The bowladrome across the courthouse lawn was busiest at lunch, the nearby Travelodge stuffed with incumbent Christs. I hate to see a crust punk hustling on behalf of a suffering pet, as though one nervous system weren't elaborate enough to bear the succulence of this privation, like one needed a proximate gullet to taunt. That's my stingy conservative talking, he lashes out at any show of friendship he can't monetize. No smoking, for example. What's that odd smell wafting off the parking lot at dusk? Omega 3's, the nutritionist said, are to your brain as oil is to a car. But that light had been on for years, unblinking so ignored. I take the bus so I can tell my story, charmless braggart ambling east. I haven't shit in Ignace in three years. It's the acoustic boogaloo that sunders you. Like playing racquetball without a wall, writing a villanelle without a line rule. Galoot forgot his hairnet, had to wear a hat. His colon killed him. Dad's cologne. A better question asked in bad faith. Who misses the Burger Family? At what point do free spirits go solo? I said that on a whim to see if we were listening. Whoever lingers longest takes the cake.

AFTER THE PARTY

The discipline of insignificance
Insists, you could be anyone's collected sense

Impression, even-handed plaint—
Misplaced the pen amid proceedings

Had to dictate to the palm
Executively. In the toilet, on the train

Tweet sweetly. I find reading
To require both hands. To knuckle under meaning

As in kneading. Any other Other, valuable
And malleable, takes an impression—

Smutty putty, wet cement. Swipe ultra-left
To second-guess variety;

Oneself. A storyboard for bedding
Allergens lining the wind

THE UNSUMMONED

"What's travel and what good is it? We never disembark from ourselves."

— Fernando Pessoa, *The Book of Disquiet*

Stage lipssh kiss the feet of banned fans
Martyrs glare in silhouette
Phone asks as I insert a SIM card
Where Are You?
* North America
* Rest of the World

↪

Abandoned homes like battlements
Flank the extension bridge—
Iron vertebrae buttress the storm
A spreading tuft of spilt milk, leiter plane

Inverts an earthen village one
Eye's length away "because I am
The size of what I see
And not the size of my stature" (Caeiro)

⤷

Orwellian owls or Aurelian walls
An All-American demesne

Or flume for traffic in a standing grid
Ghost surgeon to the dream body

Dispositif and appetite, repeating
In a fine romance . . .

⤷

For the Kava of morning
The grotto of night

A teary eye or
Tincture of alterity

Between bouts of
Bottled gratitude

Each bad case of the fidgets leases
"Human culture" to

The parking war
Or working pour

Morning or moaning
Pazi Na Svoje Stvari: (Mind Your Stuff)

⤷

Variation—Integration—Difference—Repetition
"The Haçienda must be built."

Scabrous collectivist lisps in my ringing ear—
A picked wound on the wicked world

It's not enough to have seen the words somewhere:
Try putting them in your mouth

↪

Inner culture for beginner sinners—
Do I err by my neighbour in holding my breath?
"The scent of these armpits
is an aroma finer than Prayer." (Whitman)
The practiced self-contempt of proper hygiene—
Nature cordoned by pocked acres—
Somehow requisite to filth's articulacy.
"Modesty is important for sensuality
like resistance for energy." (Soares)

↪

"Facing a Slavic soul"
It's best to follow their preferences:
The tipple most associated with
Doom culture, ergo
Googleable, chastised by peer Stasi
From across the world, a good debt
Beckoning to keep in touch.
Try thinking a language other than
Objects arranged by date.

↪

After the national-retentive phase
Make me a sluice—

Dollarized
One dons the collar.

Just desserts for the disaster tourist.
"Nothing feels as good as freedom tastes."

⤷

Two nights

Three nights

A week

Two weeks

With a bath

With a shower

With a balcony

Hot water

Running water

⤷

Though it may be an asset
In the ass-end of the theatre
Paid ascension from
The gutter in the summer

svenir cuty auf says phone
Le Monocle de Mon Cul
Sic one's credit on a scenic city
Difficulty with the kets this wend

↪

Our frenemies enframe us
Troupes amassed along the canvas
As the self is shored upon the skin—
So what's a fungus, nature in the guise of other?
Sanitation symptom of improper separation
In the common-cold war? Is a cold sore
A conjuncture on the face of it?
How does the body strike?
To what extent does your 'they'
Mean our 'us?'

↪

Brand erotism of the dispossessed
Love in a corner stall

The city an abandoned carousel
Everything closes by night

Except the bars, where everyone's
A mascot for their own desires—

An Irish pub next to
An English pub no enmity just

Different coloured chairs
Marking the patios apart

"No Nose No Hope In Here"

↪

Après la fin du monde
There is the after-party—
After the party is there politics?
Pustules erupt along the wrist
A gift of our wet mattress
Spans from sleeping spot
To seeping flesh—
Interstices between the gaps
A suppurating bliss—
Some people would reduce
The commons to a kiss, turn
Iron curtain denim corridor
God help me to survive
This deadly love

⟶

Rusted over our mobile abode
A closer tower throws the horns
"Viva el the Real"

Aloe flowers, ally of the dermis
In an oddly crowded desert, signal-
Blocking lancet in the brush—

It is incredible how quickly you forget
Without a guidebook where you are
Requesting coverage

To authenticate the thicket—
White reverberators writing
"rhythmic tears" (Soares)

↪

Fast as the heartbeat of a felled bird
On a fêted day
I heard the distant fireworks

Through vacated corridors
Of ghost-town thrift
I followed them

Onto a consecrated square whose saint
Was sat serenely on a wall
Blessing an escalating brawl

Citroën scented exhaust fills the nostrils
Lost a bet abut the mural for
Good luck

↪

Which antique taste acquires a denizen
Unsettled heft the rift to mend—

That something bigger spans the ocean
Which breadth narrows the mind.

Learn the old cities' names
And put them in your pocket—

Wherever you and your depressing freight
May travel, these will canvas in advance

Reporting home indifferently, "it never is
It's only ever what just was."

THE AFTER-PARTY

More claptrap from the apparatchik
Able-bodied but inept.

A scold called nomenklatura—
That's call-outs, collegial roasts.

If you've got beef, milk it
To stringency. If you love architecture

You have ghosts. 'No Future'
Was a Third Way, too—

The New Deal raw in those days.
Take a seat. No, really, take it

Furniture a party favour
In the aftermath of sullen company

Eviction picnic on behalf
Of planetary host—

SNOWMARE Thought I could dangle in the interval above the stair, below the street; held that our heat might keep in transit, or between two cities, separate lives—two beings represented in the moment of their knowing non-conformity to arbitrary fact. Reflexive chafe below lace tracery, umbilicus. Our every kiss a costume. Seamy seamlessness, flush feeling space may be contractible against all odds. Am I liberal in love? Define your terms. But if you haven't broken up with someone on a cellphone from a Whole Foods bathroom, you don't know the depth of bathos, yet. That night, I took him in the mouth to Whitehouse. Are we so illiberal in lust? See how the sketchy overture cancels a common debt. Watch status structure the transgression. How Democrats debate the facts as if these strictures were debatable. Rather, ask what is to be, as always, ask what is, if imprecisely, to be done, as lovers do. Am I too literal in politics? In love?

The city's wakefulness, the glitzy sky
Obliquely allied to my farthest friends

Who say, with grave concern, where were you last night, when we almost broke the record for the most pathetic reminiscence uttered sober in a dream of death?

Resounds a silence. I am varyingly each of them—
His jaw, her chin, his upper lip and voice

The way he holds his station, even as nothing is asked of him. How he clenches his fist on demand. I've known him so that any loss of detail is beside the point. His entrance to a room

Sashaying tipsily as though:

For ten years, frequenting the public record
Proper denizen of airports, I would hear the escapees' lament
That 'nothing changes' here, while I was decomposing at their feet.
Every vacancy is rumour, all is vapour—object permanence,
Procured by sleight of words, still relative to one's own fleetingness.
To leave requires an axis not a destination. Flesh can be a supple leash.
To trip centripetal across the peopled plane—miss someone, say it
To their face. Oh wait you can't. Write fan mail to said face. Forget
To send it anyway, your everyday an unremitting fog. Create
The face which, in your recollection, comes
More closely to resemble *nemesis*.

Things hate this guy, and you should too. There's nothing that he wouldn't do to make you happy—that kind of fool would rally to a bookstore for the love of books, or pledge his life to everyone at once, blank cheque to bounce in triplicate. Before I die I want to watch a crayon melt, to demonstrate against mortality. As per final instructions, place spicy nasturtiums on his grave, attracting bears. Remember, he was always late and so apologetic. Not today. We stumbled through that snowstorm lowing as our toes lost feeling; stopped to fill a phone booth with our bodies both and make a dial tone of our breath. Before I want to die I watch The Heathers sober and without reflection. A cobweb of pre-cum connects his bent appendage to my aching chin. A city is the superficial fact that we refuse to find ourselves alone. Regard the standard garb for bits of flair. An oil-sheen on the surface of your supper, a Styrofoam basin of soup. The sheets graph intervals of calm, valleys of sleep between salt icicles of fear. Throw pillows tossed and huck sheets hugged to chest. Crossword completed in two hands. Our air is dry, the chair moist with the ghost of last night's session. Lesson capably learned. Now I'm itchy with grief creeping Instagram, making everything about myself again, by the glow of your self-deprecating cenotaph, in the cool of your permanent shadow. Driving west, a sadness cresting in the chest, below the throat—

I still recall, strapped in the backseat of a car
Eyes vaulting power lines, gliding along
The slack wires sending voltage town to town.
Each time I blinked before a changing scenery
I'd call that take-away a photograph
Without a thought as to exactly where
This irrecoverable archive would appear—
I found comfort in my presumed ability
To store surroundings on command, watching
The fields pass as though already pictures.
I seldom waded into these myself
Happier counting threaded crosses through
The treated glass of safety windows. I remember
Denim pockets on the seatback, stuffed
With a day's distractions. Once it occurred
To me that this was where the photos went.

I am a lifelong passenger, riding beside
Someone, or else behind them, with affection.
I like to fiddle with the radio, one way
In which I am a child today, happily captive
And the best songs I associate with being led.
Because of this passive relationship
To transit, I'm still terrified of driving—
Every time I get into a stranger's car
Some part of me presumes an early death.
This me that dreads to leave the city, even
For an evening, is that same fanatical child
Who fears all lost when out of touch.
Ironically, I am a stalling correspondent
For the city offers its consumer feedback
In a there-and-gone game of immediacy
That tends to the nearest horizon. It distracts—

Eyes follow that unwavering line roadside,
An illusory divisor of pictorial space—
I'd stare into the cereal for swaying signs
And come up empty-handed, glassy-eyed.
So accuse me, not the landscape, of indifference
To the reel and rout of our surroundings;
Any rootedness; reality itself. Depression is a day
In which all grass is green. Elsewhere the cities
That I love enact a kind of horror vacui—
Bustle oblivious to void, an ornamental sprawl.
That said, the city's seams are showing in
The so-called countryside. Considering
The psychic ravages of this arrangement,
I plead 'prairie madness,' transient affliction
Of ex-urban colonizers new to isolation—
Exiles of trickle-down convenience.

Kid theorist of the nearest media,
Finding the depth of space already scored
According to some metronomic rule,
Staves slackening outside the city limits,
Faces the window and awaits his cue—
A cognitive percussionist whose symbol
Makes a slapstick splash upon arrival
Timed to coincide with a liquid relief.
The obvious analogy is with film—
How distance is a question of succession
And convertible to time as passage.
Then what does matter's animacy have
To say to creatural chronology—
The vehicle in which we find ourselves
Already somewhere en route? What looms ahead
Of belted being, a ballooning airbag
Of an Umwelt, panorama tempting fate?

That I learned time in Manitoba means
That time is only sometimes green. Seen
From a parking lot, time is a storefront
Keeping its own hours. Seen from above
Time is a parchment, composite of property
Already parcelled out to others. Nearer earth
Time is non-digital, a signature—
Pedestrians could bend it underfoot
And walk the days back without repetition.
A sombre child, I couldn't cede enough
Attention to the time of occupation
As a settler's vision is unfurling vistas
Of enclosed contentment, empty time
Preceding consciousness. Say I was born
Before the world in nineteen-eighty-five—
Then how much intervening since
Would be our sole responsibility?

Suppose that every creativity endorses
Those conditions it cannot negate. A colony
Is not a problem of opinion but perception,
First impressions constantly refreshing—
A repressive preciosity. This makes poetry
Complicit: new words put to old associations,
Asking pangs of recognition to outstrip
The space between different positions.
No sentimental technicality can close
The apperceptive rend of my own wake
Across the earth, a tourist from the first—
Though I remember sifting shared reality
In interested fistfuls, feeling detail, grasping
Little and demanding names; a poetry
Of sorts if not of types, lost for a plot
And knowing only lowly narrative.

Hopping from dot to dot, eyes draw the lines
That flight affirms, bracketing home; though
Any claim to an-originality misses the point,
As though it could be placed behind me.
Opting out of hospitality, short-sighted
As I am, I wouldn't flee from space—
Like a ridiculous Odysseus, astride the sea.
In Freud, "that oceanic feeling" means
Unlimited rapport with one's surroundings,
A bottomless immensity sans otherness.
We find ways to obliviate, if fleetingly
Though I've avoided these for shall we say
Cartesian reasons; an indulgent sadness
Cresting in the chest, below the throat—
So I displace myself incessantly, whence issues
The paradox that I write only from away.

Looking as driving in reverse; to leave
Is to have been for once, eventually.
Signposts remind us of each landmark
In advance of passing, rationing the map
To each dim navigator with impatience.
Probably Zeno had to pee. I'm glad to be
Here, noticing how your knees bounce
The keys, as an accompanist to road-roar
In our sonic envelope with snacks.
It's good not to destroy what isn't ours
By either imposition or forgetfulness—
Before sight-reading and close listening
Disclose the landscape as a fervent hush
There goes a subject whose desires are less
Innocuous than plain unknowing; as
A product lacking finish, and a start to
Which I'm growing closer everyday—

ROMANS In the season of gooseflesh and sweaters, every threshold is tested. For sleep, new insulation; for the windows, nearer panes. The campaign was an overlong conquest of lawns. The boulevards became our commons, under threat of picturesque dissensus. Who pickets the impending day, straddles which neighbourly barricade? The pancake batter looked like vomit, yesterday's intentions overturned into the sink. Only what kind of lunatic barfs on the dishes? One experience of poverty is to walk prodigiously, the distance to the laundromat then back, clothes damp to dry them on the fence. Total savings in brain cells and cents: about a day's rent in the afterlife. This fall, one candidate relays our information to the market. I would he were aboard a wicker basket, smeared with tears and querying constituents for mercy on behalf of his successors. Sitting fireside, I'd knit him a flag. Who reads the news and isn't turning tricoteuse? Road rage as displaced class hatred, shaking steady hands. In the suburb I grew up around, sidewalks etched with swastikas, a plot of new cement was ready-wet for propaganda. Above the fray, the people in glass houses can't use the bathroom at night: they are a lantern to the world, and we are moths to their good fortune. As art appreciates, the point of housing has become that everybody wants a home, but knows there simply aren't enough to go around. The sight of supper a scarcely believable taunt. Certain menacing themes date the text. The headless sailors are less naked than a sign. A snarl coiled in the throat, awaiting winter, a wind-bitten competition. Earplugs halve the pleasure. Whether angry-hungry or nonplussed, each of them disapproved in their own fashion. A reaction formation to finish. Is your older sister yet a soldier? Does the memory remain when you repeat? As early in the evening as half-seven, my eyes seized on the direction of the grain. As though a current gripped my ankles, I would cross the room in long diagonals, staggering north-east or south-west exclusively. I couldn't reach the bathroom. We spent three days with my feelings and came home. The candidates are two smartphones with different chargers. A generation gap commends early adoption. Eyebrow solo. Punctuation Suite. Plug awkward silence with a comet, more stopgap guffaw. I'm too effete to have a fate, and that too is a kind of theft. The coin collectors have a table in the mall on a revolving basis. That one could vote, if not strategically, then only on the maxim that one render unto Caesar what is his.

Placed last in karaoke—

Am I suspended in guffaws?

An e in any other ear, wool be as wet

And other presentations of a debt

To teachers pre-deceased—

We fête them with hate in our hearts.

Worse hallmarks than precocity

And ill-health keep me sleepless

Yet I left the conference in your lap

A scrappy pet, born to the discourse

Afresh. On a train blurring trees

Daubing branches with a damp brush

'Picturesque' the expectation

I awoke not knowing where it was—

Too many smokestacks to count

A dog in silhouette a cardboard sentry

Verdure of Jersey roadside ditches

Only certain accidents do we recall

Ages since television was a reservoir

And not a store, since God was a

Decision not a coastal storm—

We live apart from one another

But can text, a timely verb

For there is no immediate rapport

Between our particles of mourning

And here's the cause for fear—

That I'll give everything I've got

To anyone without condition

But I hate to share.

His eyes a searchlight meet my own

A mist, we make an outpost with our arms

We all place our hands on the sportsball

I hate winning I like to congratulate him

The larger part of me prefers to lose

As music sounds sweeter to those

Who live close to their goals

In perfected frustration.

The express train animates

Ads on the platform like a flip book

Actors metamorphose into

So many different coloured clothes

Before our eyes the world is changing

Maybe rapidly enough to frighten those

Who own it, those who bank on fear.

One's inner child incants 'it isn't fair'

An inner adult seethes, this isn't metaphor

Why not regress to expectation?

Too much like abandonment, the risk

In politics is that it's running down your wrist

In rivulets and into someone else's register—

Is getting by like making out?

His shoulders as a mountain shard in sleep

Rhyme of resemblance in the dark.

I miss so many people that I haven't met

But how I sing it in my dreams

Is not the waking tune, nor is it recollected—

Dimples in the dumplings, donut holes.

The poem is a phoned-in thing

Wrists burn from writing everyday

With breathless trepidation

At the crosswalk on the train in line for

Such brusque service I felt bruised for days—

The smallest things smart truly, a mute trifle

Obviates the guilt of living like a prince

Of needing coffee, non-monogamy

A living wage, and other non-relations

While the messages I should have sent

And messages to send make a roughly

Equivocal whole of all social necessity—

But I love you many Names

Each in your secrecy, soft knees

Below allusive hem, the world a quarrel

Or a sheet of wind to spit into

Is ill-advised: catches the platform air

The train ten minutes late, and counting—

SNOWMARE Nick back of neck for stinging styptic, asking antiseptic chapstick of a stranger's pocket. They all have that endangered look. The windchill is the killing thing, an extra metric nudge beyond believability and livability both. A seasonal perdition. I have never met a limit but in retrospect. Not my favourite local institution, only in the woolen autumn I could bear them overear. An itch to hear that old familiar melody inside the union hall. The singers stood half-thawed and sodden, taking history for their inheritance. One day all of this disaster kitsch—the heraldry of hockey teams, secular Christmas sweaters—will have ceased to signify. Which outer limit would you rather live inside, the strained civility of strangers or the prejudicial tics of friends and lovers? You break it if you brought it on. In Niedecker's non-benediction, it is brotherhood toward which we persist. A rubber mat for static, stomp your feet. Wand-struck about the brow, between unknowing and uncaring. Water, drivel, derivation. Are we men or Devo? Can the institution tell, or do we care? I couldn't drink enough to make the grade, not in those semeny corrals. Too many quacks and Kerouacs. Suburban Bacchus does Quebec one dive bar at a time. But then, a piece of lint suspended in a stream of piss as though by magic, dancing on a mere hair in a sparkling arc of four am relief, gave me a Lilliputian intimation of enormity. And every night I fall asleep one full hour later than the night before. More days I wake up with a stabbing pain inside my asshole, too stupid to shit. On Covert Joy Way, staring scrappily. Count teeth inside my mouth and clench. Lungs are a cavity. A cruising gait, suggestive in its hesitancy. Others swing their arms to sign indifference. Heavy mud abducting boot, in busted anonymity we sulk home, gearshift solitaire. 'Imprivacy' was your word for the canopy of longing any two extend. No vacancy invites improvisation. It's nobody's business where I put my bones. At home, abroad, or mid-course of a fake itinerary. A fly into my naked eye. What do the Finnish say especially? A strained flirtation, parching as salt licorice. Experience above the treeline is conspicuous, one's every gesture lucent with seasonal hesitancy. A new constraint: the poem must say something that the author means. Furthermore, the poem must contain the words "the poem," in the same way the Ramones or Motörhead extol the benefits of rock'n'roll. I have a feeling that you're going to like it here. Only the smallest could attend. To be noticed by another, at the intersection, by the luncheonette. Preferring language to the body, never venturing a destination.

A work beginning in silence. A world originating in the same, though never quite the same. Too often that was me, so eager to be loved that I would say the wrong thing just to know remorse. Roundtable hours, host chopping celery atop a wooden block. A field of grass for grazing—but there's something called rent. Brighter than midnight on Broadway, ginger root to therapeutically abrade the throat. Fight fire with fire, not opposite but equal. As nearby suburbs burned, our air became the second-hand equivalent of seven cigarettes. How you feel in the end is directly related to how you were feeling in the beginning. Mood lighting on a desert patio, the salad lit up in the sun. To rest transparently in other-power, also known as 'going Dutch.' Any deeper feeling needs a filter. Metadata keeps the date.

HONED POME

Awake self-same no writ effacing traces as
A blister doesn't interrupt the fingerprint
Legible all the while I'm smiling
And the rotting floorboards get to smelling
Like kombucha or some old world orderly
Intestinal confection, scarred or soiled
The ceiling. As has been said, we are
All somebody's upstairs neighbour
In this hospital of options called life—
The verb 'to be' just seems so awfully final
Like for example no one here observes
The distantly foreseeable slow death of vinyl
And our passion grows more fervid
With each pressing, moment of
Collector's indecision, packrat guilt.

Cop with a moleskine. Poet with a conscience.
Coping mechanism. Top with foreskin.
Leonard, I feel like I should see you soon.
Am I that smell? The mossy knoll
Oh that can't be my look, a lone one sulking
In a corner of the mildewed dungeon, hating it—
There Thomas had his first ever haggis.
MLM MSM seeking a further future
For the most of us apply. Then
I won't get to wear my summer cardigan
Indoors again if there's to be another season.
Say the best things in life are not things—
A store-bought ontology at best but I appreciate
Your social blunders in a world of trinkets
Moral rubble in the wrinkle blinking back

I.

lapping a ticker tape parade
of light on leaves
rutting in mud en route

an ace thwacking the spokes
or polyester usher lisping pickup
in a cartoon park—

i'd never seen so many skinheads
waiting for the bus at once
until i got to sydney

an unlovely bunch of coconuts
departing for the beach
shirts tucked in socks—

tarkovsky's stalker but the quarry
stops to fuck the con man in a quarry
verdant with discovered colour

kneeling knuckle deep in dirt
somebody made off with my bike
in silence, left the card

II.

leaving society i met a guy
living inside an orgone hangar
in latrobe   expelled from horror school
for boasting of his real intent to finish
life a figment of his own imagination
in full bloody regalia to make a film of
everything   unauthorized   immense
wherever you are ian i remember
sleeping in your moldy hammock
holding your cloaked hand

III.

brutalism is most photogenic when abandoned
on a tundra in the nineties in a book
the simulation of another earth depending on
the present gravity work shirts ascending
a corroded ladder to the stars an escalator
still as stairs a textbook favourite of the kids
raised over carpet in the crystal suburbs
where a surfeit of design draws contract
after contract nothing like a social dungeon
where to watch another's crumbling face
in close-up drastic pastures of imporous waste
the moss like stubble shoulders crumble
everybody loves an underwater palace
not apparently enough to drown the world

IV.

left everybody free
no happiness behind
i really meant it
life like being cute

asks meaning s-o-s
osmosis i knew that
from being left back
way before is was

frank messaging
a strong if small dis-
claimer social whiner
in the windowsill

a bully in the bar
tsk tsk you're here
you're really here
for real, for free—

Shooting dirty pool, shirt dipped in soup
The market flounders door
To motel door, enumerating numbheads
Nodding out for spite. What is a vote?
As sure as birth starts at conception (Melrose)
Same way opposites attract (New Munich).
You're naked, put some graphics on.

Stuck up nob creek without a puddle: two
Nude beaches on ten thousand lakes
Were crowded with the option of escape
Yet no one waded in to help, not one soul
As we passed the coastline in a cup—
The first sip tasted like a refill.
West is left and North is up.

He drove, her taurine animus
His mermaid bride across
The stateline for a prize

The highway gleamed
A gilded taint
Its fur unfurled for miles

The bit rate hobbling poplar
Musty sinusoid interior
He stood and stirred before

Head of a herm, harmed marble
Stooped arranging hair
Into an antique sign

Collapsing form and function
Bench and basket
Rain or shine

How each treats their ovoidal orb
As though light were a paste—
Slather it over yourself

What started as road rash
Clotted raspberry
Then spread—

His accomplice an insect at breakfast
Pectin spread, ingredients inspected
Save pellucid salve for scorched bread
Bland and stackable like days—

A fine mess this inseminating glaze.
Light treads across the surface
Which terrain tacks to the touch
And bucks back underfoot. The body

Is such feeble matter, feeling sponge for
Water; porous when you try to purge
What you'd intended to ignore—

To empty you upend the gorge. It's better
To content yourself with form
You winged thing, growing as a worm . . .

Wind absolves you of your hearing
Jet planes score the sky
Which cupola clears the clearing—
Stark trees tantalize the lightning
Our licentiousness creates.

Meanwhile the mainly male gaze gawks
At none of this the least endearing
And the wronged man walks
With able swagger

'WHOOSH'

Overear headphones blare
'Theme From Interiority'
This is Ethics Street the next stop
On this train is Bowery
Elbow defending solitude against
"The imposition of the chance
Community" (Schüle re: Wolf)
Well, that's one way to say
Full frontal lechery, the silly lambs
Glass nipples strewn about the floor
Here is no auditorium, stone deaf
Atop familial jelly or a mesh:

Cubules of content for a mattress
Some things you don't purchase
Such as thermal wan-ware at the
Height of summer seventh hand
'The new ephemerality'
Our shadows are as sculpture
Under a hammering sun
Hateful invariant this year
Dilating like an orifice it orbits us
Again, noses and yeses (nod to
Blau DuPlessis) in the scorching air
A bleuve groise all eye sees

And even after all these years I am
Upset at punk ethnographies
By descriptions of old friends the most
And our youthful stupidities of
Certainly myself and sundry others
Whose unlucky stars had set
By day three of proceedings that
Created them; nobody citing as in biting
(Duty *beckons*, never actually calls)
People in glass shoes don't kick stones,
Trip seldomly from home, tip
Painted toes for reinforcement:

Say 'shin splints' five times fast, say
'Please' as quickly if you can
Apparent patron to the process
Marx acquiring capital by Beuys:
Romance, we jest, is only ingestible dust
And guess which gust had just confessed
To ruffling feathered tresses
Of which guest's second-best most
Party-weathered dress? Flush plumage
By the fistful, fake distress for wet results.
More antisocial than apparent, as hot
Air reserves a poem, pre-discursive.

A portrait of the artist washing feet.
Capital as invisible sculpture.
Or, as the composer might say, dressed
In his mid-career pajamas,
"There is no such thing as silence"
Nor as pure repression, nor
Vorhanden apparatus:
Every failed rustician makes
His bluffing way into the gallery
Sooner or later, whether called out
Or collected, in the long run we
Are better read than compensated—

THE UNSUMMONED (SUMMER ABROAD)

"Travel is for those who cannot feel. That's why travel books are always so unsatisfying as books of experience."

— Fernando Pessoa, *The Book of Disquiet*

A vernacular take on a classic—
First prospectus in a public park
Our practised frolic, "nature's pop-up book"
Or wooden cross without a permit
Greening Jesus sit on it, il suffit que je foi
Waxing polemic on the lawn

The sheepscape ate him and a nearby couple:
Everybody barfed together
As a staple of the morning-after—
A jingle or nostalgic scherzo
Rises from a nearby bench
Been miserable, bien malheureuse
The pond fondled my ankles
Failed Ophelia, the afternoon in tatters

†

That the mist across the Wisła has no silhouette
No history as such, or that the vista rests
Less easily upon the water than an oil slick
May remind our visitor—the afterimage of a neon
Lody floating in her vision, tempting feint—
That not all transit is intrinsically mysterious.
Our loved ones tend to get the worst of us.
The cruise ship empties waste into its wake—
Improperly utopic, saving oxygen by banning banter.

†

When preparedness seems simply tacky, just so
Glaringly un-local, like looking at a family
Portrait through binoculars or stopping midpace
On the sidewalk to debrief; tell me, sir or Siri
Where do the parish fauna eat? And should one be
Found falling—this obsesses me—is it too late then
To swap seats? In the terminal, so many spirits
Shuttled past. They wouldn't answer my address
So I repeated slowly, with great emphasis:
"It never is, it's only ever what just was."

†

Sapped from standing room accommodations, hordes of sophomore Foucauldian archaists, elbows tucked, flood the arcades—monetized vomitoria, a hollow in the horizontal rain. A trapezoidal topper kept us on a tether. Motion sensors mutilate the face, a henceforth featureless maquette. And yet: night heightens the intensity of turquoise. Dusk elucidates the colour rust, while buskers index the irrelevance of overhearing, "compositional." Sat proudly mammal on the patio, an ideal illocality, we lost our wager with the weather. As our day's epic was restored to blotter, I could hear the laughter of the Other pelting from the eaves and knew that it was good. Two dozen lashes of the long tongue in a glassed-in room. Desire a flash-flood of the blood. A dish called Bombay Foreplay had us shitting in the sink. An evening's syzygy had not prepared us for the topic of dessert. And then descended through the park, an episode in which I blanch at any precedent. A shaved head bobbing on a sidewalk, calves like daggers, luminescent laces like bared teeth. At home I see a mirror and am ashamed to fear my neighbour as I ought to fear myself. Our bodies are at market, I don't know my own strength or extension; which, it turns out, is my greatest strength.

†

But it had been an education, nights inhaling cumulus
Of wiseacre dissension, dropping to our knees in prayer
So often I could stand to swap out patella for bounce—
A better penitence depends upon it. Could I live there
On a barely sloping plane? A parapet is for the birds
The crumpled waiver in my pocket for assurance—
That there are greater things than words, to which words
Happily defer. The first trait lost is atmosphere.
The second, innocence. The third, meaning, is worst
To live without; once béton brut but lately wet cement.

†

Under Phrygian cap I strut my stratum: to slam
The belching smelter door, must one first span
The breadth of its frame? Mind the Fregean gap
Between prole and factotum; modal frontage
Flouts a name. Party tricks of a prodigal Dauphin—
To dance on the head of pin, rinse and repent
Or starve oneself to slither through the needle's eye.
People sleep as the body requires it, in fits.

Cold feet about to give us both the boot
Are muddying the flophouse floor. For forty days
And fewer nights, not counting smoke breaks
We laboured together to set the historical stage
Admiring them at first, the grandiloquent ones—
This kind of group crush straightens by consensus
Thus it crushed us, a tremendous pestle of
Unspent love, our Germanic will to powder.

†

Still today I salivate to hear the rustle of a belt
Behind paper-thin walls, a whisper through the curtain—
"What I enjoyed about these vast fields
I enjoyed because I don't live here," Soares says
A shunt the continent; exeunt

†

A clit is not a carousel. A cock is not an icicle.
But for a certain brand of frisky humanist
The anus is denominator.
Not the most sentimental interior
She said, tickling the keys.
Or does one wiggle on it? There is agency in inability.
There are excuses for unwillingness.
That, to me, looks like a bunch of sticks.
Wryly appealing, pick your own leaky mentor:

I learned Poetry from Lego. Non-discursive.
A pre-genital fidget makes a virtue of
His lifelong abstinence from politics, from
Speech, while AEIOU spells love as well.
(DESPITE EFFECTIVENESS)
The Creaky Arts Knee Ruffled Moffatt 'For the Win'
Say every play includes a wedding, that's a thesis.
Which depends upon your definition.
Yes, and? – Ditto, nope.

As destiny descends a glowing string
Do something daily without forethought.
It was a bad decision, loving stranger
Didn’t really need the change of address
And his last attempt to loom seductively across
Our vacant gaze without protective pince-
Nez, that I could never pronounce
Ended in dire humiliation—
Moist skin dragged across a coarser page.

Frot the lot of them. Compiling dustpan
Of stray elementals, guild on guild build us
A boardroom on the concourse of
A shoes-and-sandals downtown—
A beguiling rebeginning for the business class
For plot-driven arrivistes
For langpo professorial for all the sleepyheads
And under-anarchists appointing absence
To the longue durée cordon your tongue

SNOWMARE New Canadians learning to curl. Sprechstimme, loose nerves. Natural light makes the complexion ache. The tick had not yet burrowed to a point of great concern. He never really felt at home there but he stayed seventeen years. That's seventeen summers, sixteen Christmases; two marriages, one job. The facts as often tell us nothing. Who can't sleep for a fear of flying in their own bed? It's not prudent to be cautious. Indoor voices, hisses discipline. The Soul, as is established, loves to play. Chordal accompaniment or Book of Changes? At its backdated basis, our existence is just gas. Sock-footed for the static thrill of winter. Day one, no nemesis. Vest weather a mild nuisance. Window shoppers skim a neon reef by night. Posh fear in lights. The customer's account had been credited twice. "I can't stand to see someone who's counted as a body on a job. Just don't be there. As long as you're there ..." Entrails, circuitry. You're giving me a complex. We have all the music in the world. On the Sunday of life, we sit and listen. Like any city, we call growth around the outskirts sprawl, for its measure is more of the same. Repetition without difference. Accumulation without qualitative change—fad diet as paradigm. It shouldn't be this hard to find a place to piss outdoors. Then only shame prevents it. No one lives here anymore, we all serially rent. My other casa is a suitcase. Uninsurable, the sum that is a city will remain. An idée fixe, wrought upon water, balanced on a spine. A gaseous cipher on the river. Sifting wreckage, lick a shifter. You can turn one inside out and it still works. The kind of pundit who encounters the Koran as Penguin Classic. I didn't stop to wonder what the evening paper meant precisely. On Jane Jacobs Way, 'mixed use' means open bars and closed banks, or the opposite. At the groin of two rivers, a dock. A sanctioned make-out spot, already stolen. I lack the libido to write city poems, like I lack the knack for daily work. A cab driver emptying a Gatorade bottle of urine at a red light. We are so many woven bags of water. Body politic as bubble wrap; a trod-upon analogy, the map and parchment separate planes. One issue is the flesh, a viscous grid pending discussion. The blueprint grows vertical blocks, a bargain tropics. His writing is like vegan baking, dry and dense. His desserts, however, have the dignity of daring. Stalling at the till to prolong the flirtation. Pretending to text in a crowd. Don't be a creep. Is cruelty a customer service? In the city, you soon learn that any landmark you can't see must be behind you. Surrounded by photographers,
try to eat shamelessly outdoors. How many ads have featured a

flag billowing as background? Dog walking on Lafayette, sensual shivers before billboard. Bowie died. I had a funny feeling. Lit upon the bridge's filigree, a straying fortress, watching the people improvise beneath my feet. Between "the romantic conception of society as an organism and the baroque conception of the organism as a society"(Chunglin Kwa) exists the city. Inside this maze are many like myself. Then at its center, there is only one of both of us.

For Kevin Killian

This book would not exist in its present form without Irene Bindi's incisive reading, for which I am truly fortunate. These texts were thoughtfully edited and remarked upon over the years by Bonnie-May Wadien, Colin Smith, Janelle Trenaman, Janis Maudlin, Joel Robert Ferguson, Kay Gabriel, Kevin Killian, Mia Kang, and Stéphane Doucet, not to mention those who published excerpts and engaged before and after readings.

The list of people who have somehow influenced this book over the time of its writing would, if adequately annotated, surpass the poem in length. I'm grateful for Ada Smailbegovic, Adam Done, Adjua Gargi Nzinga Greaves, Alex Snukal, Alex Stearns, Allison Glasgow, Amye McCarther, Ana Speranza, Andrea Actis, Andrea Roberts, Andrea Bell Stuart, Andrew Klobucar, Andy Robinson, Angela Forget, Angela Lopes, Anju Singh, Anna Gurton-Wachter, Anna Kreienberg, Ashleigh Bryant Phillips, Asiya Wadud, Beth Popham, Billy Hough, Brad Skibinsky, Bret Parenteau, Brittany Dennison, Bronwyn Dobchuk-Land, Buck Doyle, Bud Smith, Callie Garnett, Candice Giesbrecht, Carl Annarummo, Carly Dashiell, Carol Isaac, Casey Plett, Catriona Strang, Caycie Soke, Celina Su, Charlie Markbreiter, Cheryl Pearl Sucher, Chimwemwe Undi, Chris Macalino, Christina Chalmers, Cindy Ma, Claire Donato, Colin Adams, Colin Popham, Corina Copp, Courtney Kavanagh, Craig Boychuk, crys cole, Curran Farris, Damien Ferland, Dan Adleman, Dan Poppick, Dan Ryckman, Dane Allard, Danielle LaFrance, Darcy Bunio, David Buuck, David Hobbs, David Glickman, David W. Pritchard, Deanna Radford, Denise Enck, Dennis Cooper, Derek McCormack, Devon Arthur, Dodie Bellamy, Donato Mancini, Doreen Girard, Dorothy Trujillo Lusk, Douglas Singleton, Drew Johnston, Elæ, Emily Janakiram, Eric Schmaltz, Evan Calder Williams, Gabriel Cruis, Gleb Wilson, Guy Bannister, hannah_g, Hayden Bennett, Ian Dreiblatt, Ian Hatcher, Jacob Becker, Jacob Harring, Jacob Schreier, James Davidson, Janique Vigier, Jared McKetiak, Jason Penner, Jason Stefanik, Javier Molea, Jay Gaunt, Jeff Onizak, Jennifer Stoever, Jesse Hill, Jessica Evans, Joe Warkentin, Joel Mierau, John Toews, Jonathan Ball, Jordy Rosenberg, Josef Estabrooks, Joseph Gerbasi, Joseph Grantham, Josh Landes, Kailey Protulipac, Kate MacNeill, Keith LaVecchia, Kelsey Braun, Kendra Place, Kevin Davies, Kevin Cassem, Kevin Lo, Kevin Strang, Kristian Enright, Kurt Newman, Landon Gray Mitchell, Laurel Squadron, Leanne Grieves, Liam Carpenter-Urquhart, Liam O'Brien,

Liv Rahel Schwenk, Madeleine Watts, Mallory Amirault, Margaret Saul, Mariana Muñoz Gomez, Marie-France Hollier, Matt Longabucco, Matt Pieknik, Maxine Gordon, Maya Bjornson, Mercedes Eng, Meredith Graves, Michael Barnholden, Michael Elves, Mike Requeima, Mike Ryckman, Mitch Dixon, Mitsuhiro Kawano, Monika Vrečar, Morgan Paradis, Morgan Peniuta, Naomi Woo, Natasha Havrilenko, Neil Bazan, Nick Murray, Noor Bhangu, Nora Kipnis, Oliver Kellhammer, Owen Toews, Patrick Grzelewski, Patrick Short, Paul Lukeman, Paul Phillips, Rachael Guynn Wilson, Rachel Valinsky, Rami Karim, Reg Johanson, Robert Taite, Roger Pantano, Rosario Inés, Rowan Moyes, Ryan Simmons, Ryan Trudeau, Rylee Lyman, Sara Jane Stoner, Sarah McEachern, Sarah McNally, Sasha Amaya, Shimby Zegeye-Gebrehiwot, Shuja Haider, Simone Mahrenholz, Skelley Blackley, Stephanie LaCava, Stephen Ira, steve dalachinsky, Stu Watson, Suzanne Goldenberg, Talitha Kearey, Taylor Engel, Teddy Zegeye-Gebrehiwot, Thora Siemsen, Toby Altman, Todd Besant, Todd Bruce, Tom Kohut, Trish Salah, Tyson Shwaluk, Valerie Slaughter, Veronika Reichl, Wayne Serebrin, Wendy Lotterman, Will Keyes, Yuko Otomo, Yvonne Brooks, Zachary LaMalfa. I hope not to have missed too many people in compiling this list.

An unending thank you to my parents, Bruce and Lynn Popham.

These poems were composed in numerous cities around the world but finally assembled on Treaty 1 territory, the traditional lands of the Anishinaabeg, Cree, Oji-Cree, Dakota, and Dene peoples, and the homeland of the Métis Nation. I'm thankful for all I continue to learn here.

Cam Scott is a poet, critic, and non-musician. His chapbook, **WRESTLERS**, was published by Greying Ghost in 2017.

ROMA

SNOWM